Rhymes Against Ruins

(From "Fault Lines" …
to "The Would-Be King")

Joseph G. Ramsey

ISBN: 978-1-967022-94-6

Fomite
Burlingon, VT
fomitepress.com

"Homo sum, humani nihil a me alienum puto"

"I am human, and nothing human is alien to me."

-Terence, African Roman playwright,
and former slave

On Bombings and Apologies

"I'm sorry," said the captain
After killing your wife
Upon maiming your children
And wrecking your life.

"I'm sorry," he said,
"The missile, it missed,"
Then took a step back
when he sensed a clenched fist.

"That damn missile went left
when it should have gone right
—It's so hard to see straight
in the middle of the night."

"Dear Sir, know our country
did not want *you* dead.
That missile was meant
for your *neighbor* instead."

When All is Said and Done (Part 1)
(2:30 am, 1/24/25)

Ok, we may not win this one.

But when it all is said and done
And History is read by none,
Like when the Earth rejoins the Sun
And God himself, though just pretend,
Will close the tale of earthly end,
And His great non-existent look
Will gaze upon the parted book
Where it all turned bad and led to doom
—A day that may be coming soon:

That chapter, paragraph, and line,
Those clear-cut marks of human time,
That sentence where the trap snapped shut
And hope went out of every gut,
When, alien-observed from Mars,
by betting robots counting cars
And carbon molecules and guns
And prison cells and wars begun
To help make sure a contract's won,
And Fires raging in the West
And ICE storms choking human chests;

Yes, when imaginary gamblers
Dealing with their cosmic handlers
Proclaim the Earthlings fate is sealed,
With not one chance left to reveal,
And pay up all their botcoin bets
Across the table—*check mate* set!—
Yes, when the gig of Earth is up,
the die is cast, the deal is done,

the Moon fried orange by the Sun
And all our promise gone at last…

Upon that page that billions wrote
The long and winding human quote,
The log of struggle, the tale of might,
and how our golden day turned night,
And how this deep blue speck went black
Because we could not find a way
To shake the boss from off our back…
Until it all collapsed:

In that compound human chapter
Tracing every single factor,
In that sentence, *yours* alone—
Yes, *YOU* there in your human home—
burning up your private flame—
its precious heat and light—*YOUR* name:
Where will it be in that lost song?
Your voice be heard before the gong?
Yes, in the book that none will read,
On scrolls torched white by galactic greed,
Where will *your name* be in that book?
What was the deed? the chance you took?
Or didn't take. Or didn't bother.
And let them take
The newborn's father?

When all of humankind went gone:
Earthling, which side were you on?

On Being Human

Right now
Somewhere
South of here
Someone is breaking the law:
Sneaking out into the desert
—trespassing private property
cutting through government wire
ingeniously avoiding ICE agents
and National Guard units
who stand spitting tobacco juice and
cradling sub-machine guns —
travelling unnoticed
without proper papers
for miles and miles
delivering   jugs of water
to discreet locations
where the North-bound
—"border crossers"—
—" illegal aliens"—
may find them
crack them open
and drink their fill,
and thereby not   become
so dehydrated
so overheated
as to die
in the dust
(nor so desperate
as to lose faith
in   humanity
altogether).

Beside the bottles   I've heard
these bearers of water plant
small red flags in the sand,
knee-high markers that can only be seen
By those who are thirsty
and know   where to look.

If you would ask these water-bearers to stop
If you would make them stop
If you would give aid to those who would
stop them,
If you are the kind of person who would force
these guardians
to disown their adopted cousins
and let them die,
clasping cacti thorns in the skeleton desert
Then I say it's you
Who must be stopped.

Perhaps it is you who should be cast out
Into the desert.

You who are the Alien
In our human midst.

What human being can feel safe
With the likes of you around?

To Kill the Bees

Dressed up in camouflage
Like soldiers
We used to hunt bumblebees in the back yard.
We would chase the bees away (or try to),
From the cement basement foot of the little red
house
where my parents tried to grow strawberries,
all the way across the clover patch that lined the
driveway.
I guess it was only a few adult steps, really.
But to us it seemed like a wide stretch of terrain:
A battlefield occupied by the enemy.
My best-friend Andrew and I—we shared the
very same birthday, us too—
We'd gather up rocks and sticks that felt like
logs—battering rams in our child hands–
And we'd gather our giddy kid courage,
tucked around the corner
a commando team on a mission:
to kill the bees.

We'd count to Three and then we'd yell
"Charge!" and aim as we ran and we'd throw
our clumsy load in the general direction of the
bee-spotted clover patch, sticks and stones tum-
bling into the air buzzing with adrenaline and
we'd keep on running—breathing hard—right
back behind the house and across the yard, far
away and safe from any bumblebee counter-at-
tack.
Recovering, huddled, we'd try to see if we'd
done any damage.
Then we'd sneak back to the woodsy part of the
yard, to gather up more sticks. For the next
attack.

I can't confirm that we ever actually killed one.
Maybe we did. Maybe we didn't.
We certainly tried.
We didn't count corpses, not that I recall.
But hiding against the house, we convinced
ourselves that we had at least sent those bees a
message that they would not forget.
High on a weird kind of hunter's rush and
swapping war stories.
Warriors.
Committed to the cause.

The bees, of course, always came back.
I think we assumed they would.
This was a war that would go on for all eternity:
Indian and Buffalo, though we weren't out to
eat them.

Miraculously, we never got stung—
(Is it really true that bumble bees don't sting?)
Nor did we break any toes on dropped logs.
The bees were tolerant of our childish, stupid
game.
Or maybe we were just lucky.

But ever since, I've had the creeping feeling that
the bees would have their revenge.

*

The sound of apocalypse, scientists are saying,
may not be that of a meteor crashing into earth.
Not a volcano erupting in downtown LA.
Not a giant wave crashing on all the coasts at
once.
Not a ring of hydrogen bombs exploding above
our heads (Though still certainly possible).
The sound of apocalypse may not be
a *sound* at all.

But a silence,
where the buzz of bees wings
used to be.

For it's not just little kid hands and little kid
weapons that the bees have to worry about these days.
The biggest of the big adults are in this campaign
with their voracious corporations and the latest
pesticide smog,
their hack and slash cookie cutter real estate,
and pest-repellant corn to feed to hogs.
They have bottom lines for battering rams
and blow-torches to illuminate their blind
forward charge–
a star-spangled electromagnetic hurricane.

Three decades later, the odds shift:

   We are learning that
   Bees don't always come back.

Yes, there's still a battle on for the clover patch
and its part of a planetary, worldwide class war.

   This time I'm on the side of the bees.

"One Promise, Kept"
(Upon hearing firecrackers celebrating the news of
Osama Bin Laden's assassination, May 2011)

Yes, America, we can still offer you up
a death
after all these years:
A glorious kill
For all your patience and persistence,
suffering and sacrifice,
(for half your taxes, ten million airport pat-
downs, a stadium full of hometown boys
Cut to shreds, and all those human stains on
your nice clean boots):
Yes, we can still make good
on a promise,
Still bring home to you that sweet spectacle:
Revenge.
(Not your son, it's true.) But at least
this digitized dream:
a Special Forces play-by-play,
a broadcast autopsy
To warm your red, white, blue toes by.

In America, anything is possible.
Are you not impressed?
Does the site of these sublime wounds not bleed
joy
Right into your skipping heart?
Does your tongue not swell with spit
and does your throat not long to gargle
on that distant mountain blood
like popped champagne?
Patriot pulses quicken, eagle spirits rise
Tugged by the dusty beards
Of skeletons
rattling across mountain tops.

Have faith, America,
Yes. We. Can.
Still. Kill. Man (andwomanandboyandgirl)
and keep promises, too, yes:
Maybe not those concerning Education, or
Work,
Equality, or Healthcare
Or life that Means something...
But we can still deliver on corpses
And that's not nothing,
is it?

So when you're feeling low
Know this:
We are there to buffer and to buoy you up
With bodies blown apart.
Bombs can blast the paint off the canvas
and give us a fresh start,
In the name of God,
In the shadow of new tomb-towers
blocking out the sun
And all that is sacred
Of America and
doesn't everybody love a good show
and a party too?
Amen
to that.

FAULT LINES:
Haiti, Two Years After
(January 2012)

I

The Earth has kept on traveling round the Sun
Since the day it shook and pulled them down.
Down
       Down
             and Down
Everything fell:
Shacks and church pews smashed through
sewers;
Palace collapsed—
                  an empty shell.
Three hundred thousand (counted, fewer.
Thousands buried,
never found).

Whole worlds ruptured; catacombs
Unleashing walled up winds of hell.

La Terre Tremble.

II

Will we forget what that shaking ground
Revealed for all to see, who cared to look?
The way the streets filled up with bloated bodies;
The way the troops drove on and let them cook?
The 'Aid' delayed, as if for fear of zombies
rising from their rubble graves to run–
White eyes blazing bloody memories
of how white masters came and took by gun.

And yet, and yet, poor Haitians did not riot--
     worked to pull each other from the ruins.

Carried those who died, and those who wouldn't
for a while,
And those who lived.

Gave until they had no more
to give.

(Meanwhile, "Security," guns in hand;
Guarding gates that no longer stand,
Protecting property of those in command.)

III

A sudden eruption
of broken heart blisters
oozing, drying on Live TV
far flung news anchors aim for the ripe wound,
peeling it back, letting us see,
seek the perfect angle
to capture
that "inexplicable-horror-of-it-all,"
(with just a dash of sugared hope thrown in for
the folks at home)
that juicy spot where the latex glove meets the
bandage
meets the hand
meets the ballot box
meets the sky.
Where it hurts to look. Where it makes you cry.
        (But never lets you find out *How* or
Why?)

From this fastened hook
America hangs
Prepared to unleash its charity thang.
Solemn Celebrities claim center stage:
And all that sit are moved.
Millions shut their eyes in prayer

(secretly thankful that they're not there)
Yet ready to do what good people should:
for a minute, an hour, or even a week.
       Never though letting the Haitians speak.

What do the people there have to say?
When they look at US what do they see?
Who will dare to take a peek today?

Caught in the sun, the pocked eye turns away.

How much can the blinded stand to see?
Band-aids slap where barricades should be.

IV

Worldwide
They say there are a dozen cities
With at least a million people each
Lying, waiting, sleeping on a fault line
(Slum-dweller flesh to feed the breach).

For each year, the Earth, it shivers
In the endless cold of space;
Quakes and quivers, like an ox
whose skin
must knock flies from its face.

The fault is not the moving Earth's
–We know that quakes will come, and even where–

At fault:
a world-wide class affliction
Razing mounds
of contradiction;
Bubbling boils that bust through skin,
Seeping hot pus, sweat and blood —
and liquid gold

16

That trickles up to rulers' lips ice cold.
Parasites suck membranes thin:
Vulture claws cleave crater-trails,
Until all precious flesh is drawn
In scabs and scars
to fit the scales:

(Heed the bankers' dark command)

               Plow the farmers off the land
               Build estates on bone and sand.
               Spill the poor in pavement cracks.
                      Stitch the work-
ers into seams
             For rulers' flowing cloaks
                  —Breaking their backs—
           letting them choke
               gasping for air–
               stripping them down to
their dreams,
               then bare.

           The earth, we know, will quiver;
               the brittled surface--
                   tear.

V

This predator's plague has no plan
for poor people,
except for the juice
to be squeezed
from their veins
         to quench its viral thirst.

Markets pressure
and hearts burst.

So long as endless profit reigns.

(The heads of state remain aloof:
Crisis = opportunity, after all
Helicopter blades
give the world a roof.
And there's plenty of sweat to catch,
as they fall.)

VI

Outside Port au Prince:
Refugee Cities–
Rain-soaked sheets
Flap on and on,
        But only the bugs and bats can fly.

The people gathering, grasp at
        Why.
Eyes peer out through fraying holes;
Fingers point: jet-liners
                tearing the sky.

Aboard   corporate   planes:
Thirsting agents
Ties loosened,
Clinking drinks in hand,
Toast to the future they bury   behind,
Traveling home,
to milder climes:

If they look down
        through parting clouds–
see only some
dirty laundry lines.

FAULT LINES PART 2

Sun and Bone
In Camp Corail (2010)

On the hot white plains
Of Camp Corail,
Between mountains and mountains
Where a railroad no longer runs
And trees no longer grow,
The state no longer dumps
the dead;
       They dump the living there instead.

Shards of skeletons are hidden beneath
Acres of crushed stone
Pressed flat as a leaf
      so flat
      it's like an army of bulldozers
      has come
      and gone in the night.

A sky-to-sky concrete plateau:
The stone mixed in with the bone below
burning the feet and blinding the eyes
of those who stand in the sun.
Even in shoes it hurts to walk;
      But it's too hot to run.

      *

It is not the earth that moved them here
but those who said they came to 'help'
who deemed their old survivor camp—
on the edge of the crumbling city shelf
amidst the debris of the walls and streets
that had soaked up their cries of joy and pain,
where at least what torn ground still remained
to break their fall was ground they *knew*—"unfit."

That place not far from the parliament,
And the flattened factory where some had
worked,
This place they had squatted on, made their own
though hardly a place to be called a home
—this strip—
was pronounced a "high risk zone."

According to experts
In human resettlement
The spot was at risk of being affected
By outbreaks: of social unrest,
communicable disease,
And perhaps fire.
        It would not do.

And so
On advice of the foreign experts
the police
batons in hand
encouraged the people to leave
        For their own good.

The former killing field
Far from the city
Would do nicely,
was thought to be more suitable,
a safer place to put them--
Though safer for whom
Was not entirely clear to the people
As they broiled, blinded by
the stone-and-bone reflected sun.

Trucks brought them there by the hundreds,
Thousands. Brought them here,
until Camp Corail was filled.

And so now

The white tents of those who still live
Informally mark the graves
of the numberless dead
never given a proper burial.

Dumped in the middle of the hidden wastes
The living dead infuse this place.
The living haunted
by the ghosts below
The ghosts, by the living above--
        They have been here for more than three
months now.
        They have been here for almost thirty
years now.

Past and present knot and gnaw.
In the heat, buried dreams
        Long sealed: thaw.

        *

After the sun goes down
the ground cools enough to walk about:
a child slips out of a tent
to dig with her bare hands
in the rocky sand. She picks her plot with a
careful eye.
Drops to her knees and scratches to get her start
Breaking up the sun-sealed crypt of crust.
It gives, but not before it draws blood
From her fingernails. She licks the wound
And spits the dirt. And digs.
        Down through the bleached, chalky rock
        Digs: searching for cooler dirt; *she digs*,
though the surface hurts her knuckles, *digs*
        Looking for dirt that will hold together.
        She finds,
hand by handful,
only still more pebbles   and more dry

dust; nothing
        that sticks
nothing
        that can be salvaged
        for making
                anything
                not even the smallest
mud castle, or ball.
Not even a good dirt cake.

She is about to give up, hands gray with dust
                but keeps on just
        a bit longer, just for the feel of it:
at least this deeper dirt is cool.
Perhaps at least-she has come so far now--
she will dig a hole big enough for her to
slip into. Like a womb. A tomb. A shelter. A
place to soak up the cool.
Her own private pool.
Her means become her ends;
                        At the very least
                she will have a hole.

But then this:
A knee and half-a-thigh deep, her eyes fix on
                        Something:

                the hard frozen flower
of a human
vertebrae (though she does not know what
exactly it is):
A weathered star of scattered backbone.
She picks it up.
        She can tell it is not stone.
—it does not fit in with the crater of dust.

It must be from somewhere else.

It must.
                    -And, look, there is another.

Like splinters, shards of history
working their way up to the surface
(almost as if the land had purpose):
The trace of some ancient species long gone,
The fossil of one who refused to go along.

The child holds the curious talisman up,
catching the moonlight
In her palm's cup.
She does not know what it is,
Only how it feels,
Different from the pebbles and stones she
usually steals
from this jagged ground.

Bringing the bone, like a pick to her lips,
She rubs it against them, as if to strum some
forgotten tune,
Some melody she has not yet been taught.
Sifting through names of extinct things.
          Is it a piece of a dinosaur tooth?

As she touches her tongue
to the very tip of her find
She hears a shriek rip through the night:

          A dozen rows of tent away:
          the rusty teeth of the gnawing saw
          Spit fresh blood on the white rock floor.

Held down by hands, a mother faints
from pain,
leaving another child alone, standing by the door.
Watching her in the lamp light.

One more landless peasant will walk no more
On her own two legs. The surgeon works quickly
While she is unconscious. *Back and forth.*
Echoes of hundreds of limbs that have come
before. Feet and arms piled on the floor.
Back and forth.

(The gangrene started in her toe.
They should have caught it long ago.)

The canvas sides, the surgeon's mask
soak up her groans and gasps
As does the rock (and the bone) below.
Thank god these flapping walls can't talk--

Nor could the splattered stone:

No one will know.

Just before morning, the mother wakes;
her invisible leg on fire, she quakes.
A strong patient, she has survived the worst.
(Yet how can it be that her foot still hurts?)
Summons up what courage she commands.
Her hands are tied to the bed with bands.
Grinds her teeth to bring the rain;
--nothing but Motrin for such hot pain.
Makes fists out of her praying hands:
> *It's hard to believe they've not been cursed;*
> *This blighted, blackened, branded land.*
> *She wishes to God that the clouds would burst*
> *And end this devil's plan--*
> *Just wash them all away-*
> *Lacking a place to stand.*

How will she endure this endless test
upon the searing desert sand?
> *The water well is half a mile away.*

Her son hears her waking cries, ducks in.
Brings with him a paper fan.
In hopes of doing something that can help
His mother.

*

On the edge of Camp Corail
The girl with the newfound dinosaur tooth
Lies in her trench,
her ancient secret gripped
in her warrior's hand.

Between her fingers and her thumb,
she turns the bone-shard into a gun;
Yes, with it she'll shoot
The rising sun.

She tightens her lip
closes one eye:
Aims at the blood-rimmed
base of the sky.

It's worth a try.

FAULT LINES PART 3

What is Needed
Campside (based on true events)

1.
In Haiti
there is money to build
walls
not to house
the poor
but to block them
from view;
to lay brick
high and thick,
not to protect
the homeless
from the elements,
but to protect
the rich man's twenty-acre
estate
from the sewage that flows
downhill
from the camp
when it rains.
And so now
when it rains
A human stew
Bubbles backs from the base of the wall
into the camp—
deep enough to drown in:
A gathering cesspool
for mosquitos
to breed
and cholera
to bloom.

2.

The construction project
Gives at least
a few men
—from another camp across town—
work:
hard, back-breaking work
for a few weeks
At almost three times the minimum wage
Of a dollar a day.
The wall at least
gives
the mosquitos
a home.

These fiends thrive,
Lay their eggs in the stagnant water
Feeding by night
on what flesh they can puncture.

Each little blood-sucker's life
is short.
They live for only a few weeks
Before they drop somewhere
Dead
In some unmarked speck grave—that is
if they aren't caught first
Between the finger and the thumb—*pffff*
They burst like tiny rotten berries.

Yes, any single
mosquito can be easily dealt with.
Once you know where exactly its buzz
Comes from.
Splat.

But in their uncountable numbers,
an invisible, everywhere swarm

They appear utterly
unvanquishable.
You go mad at night
just swatting the sound of them.
Praying through razed blisters
for someone
to drain the godforsaken swamp.

3.
Across the street, *Food for the Poor* (that's their name)
Tells a delegation from the camp (they're next door neighbors)
that they cannot help them;
That this is a not a distribution center;
That FFP's funds go elsewhere
And that, besides, they wouldn't want to start trouble by
giving food (or mosquito netting)
to people
Just like that,
Without, you know, going through all the proper channels.
Without armed guards present
to keep order
and paid clerks on hand
to track everything on official charts and checklists:
how many grains of how much rice went to whom
and to where and what color it was, and who said
please and who thank you (and who did not).

I mean, if distributing food to the poor was as easy as, you know, just
Givingfoodtopoorpeoplewhosaytheyarehungry
andwhohavetheribsandcollarbonestoproveit
then, well,
You wouldn't even *need* professional

organizations like
Food for the Poor
in the first place,
would you?

4.
A world away
Far beyond even the locked gates of Charity
Elsewhere
Where "History" is made
A UN official
gets promoted
to stand behind a podium and
speak of "A risk of a pandemic" and
"A surge in infant mortality."
Earnest euphemism
Rolls off that juicy pink tongue;
(The fluent official gargles water
Before coming on stage
with another bottle of *Aquafina* at the podium
Just in case
the throat suddenly dries up;
It can get so hot up there,
Under all those bright lights,
With all the world watching.)

5.
Meanwhile
In the dark
cholera stretches its limbs across prison floors
From steel barred windows to crack-webbed walls
Where profane protests against the state
are smeared in shit
and blood. Some walls still won't fall,
As more are planned.

*

Tons upon tons of construction materials
Sit piled at camp-side:
Metal beams like the stacked legs of starved giants,
Head-high mounds of sand and crushed granite,
rubble
Fresh-shoveled and trucked
from the wreckage of Port-au-Prince.
(Fortunes to be made in the sale of rubble.)

Monster machines sit idle. Watched over by
armed guards.
And a handful of hired workers stand and
smoke, idle too,
waiting to break ground, at the boss's order.
Their muscles itch for work.
There are building materials here
for a hundred homes, at least.

Only,
Not.
The homeless are not to be housed.

The squatters are to be
Evicted
from their road-side camp
By the rightful land owner
With the official stamp.

He wants to build a factory
He *needs* to build a factory
—*there is money for a factory*—
obligations to meet
words to keep
(The owners, too, imprisoned, by what they
must build
Though their jail-cells are air-conditioned,
fine coats keep off the chill.)

There's a signed contract with a foreign company
to produce: *Baseballs*
to be exported and sold to Sporting Goods stores
who will sell them at a mark-up
to the parents of little American boys and girls
who have fields to play in
and who can afford to lose things
in streams and under fences
and buy new ones.

6.
Campside
Hundreds of people contemplate
Scraping up the will
to struggle together, to keep their grip
on a cracked plot of ground that they never
asked for
In the first place;
That was forced upon them:
A sun-baked tarp-town
where they have been confined for more than a
year now,
without schools or sanitation,
While the rulers make plans
That do not include them
Except as sources of
excrement
To be sealed off
Or else
cheap labor
to be mixed
with the bricks
that wall people in
and people out.

*

The bulldozers rumble
The manager shouts
"If there's no trouble, if you all move out,
Some of you may get the chance to sew baseballs.
You like baseballs, don't you?"
The new boss promises two dollars a day.

A few will be hired—the rest
Flushed away.

7.
Will the refuse of this system pick this city
of sheets and boiling shade
Of ghosts and newborns and grandparents
and toys
But no safe place to play and
Of grime and sand
and whispered rebel songs
And blanched memory
To make their stand?

The stagnant wastewater by the wall
rises.
Do they think they can?

Or will the machetes and machine guns
scatter them in the night
(As they have done before)
Leaving them in the ditch
Dreaming of clean streams,
a plot of land,
And a world
That's been flushed
of walls
and the
rich?

8.
A rash spreads across the old woman's legs.
What can she do
But bang her two pots together at half past noon
with the others,
(a daily demonstration)
that, and be ready to place her body between
her grandchild
and the bulldozer, when they come?

She's lost her shop, and her sewing machine.
Used to sew clothes for people in the city,
To patch the garments of those who could not
afford to buy new.
(She had been one of the luckier few.)

There is plenty here that needs stitching.
By hand, she does what she can do.
sews rags into a quilt,
keeps a sole
on a shoe.
(Plenty that needs tearing down, here, too.)

*

A baby lies asleep on the bed,
a mosquito net dome, laid over his head.
Those elsewhere who can afford it use mesh like this
to protect their finger sandwiches from the flies,
when they sit out with guests in summertime.

*

In an alley of the cramped camp
The braids of a child
Flap in the wind
As she chases a red rubber ball downhill
Between tents
Trying to catch it

Catch
it
Before it rolls into
the muck.

*

Do you want to know
What happens next?
Do you?
Or shall we just let this one go, too?
Let it go
Let it go
How much of this world are we willing to just
Let go?
How much humanity
Will we just let go
Let fall away
Like some ball
slipping through
A child's open palm?

Or a kite forever swallowed by the sky?

*

Fresh watered flowers
and incense torches
line the owners' oblivious porches,
keeping off the bugs,
masking some distant stench.

And a young girl has drowned in a rain-swollen
trench.

*

There is money in Haiti
To build with; it pours in;
the rich hire poor people with it
erect walls with it
so they don't have to see
the sludge
That soils their green gardens.

And this too:
so the sorrow-sick souls gathered now
by the edge of the camp-side mire
still gripping pots and pans
unearthing and wiping clear the braided face of
the child
Can't see them, the rich,
sitting there in their place
out in the sun, doing what they do,
Enjoying the open air:
So well-dressed,
carefree
            And so few.

More than a million still homeless in Haiti.
It's not for lack of brick or steel
nor engineers
Nor hands to build with.
Not for a lack of land.
Not for a lack of money.
Not for lack of a Master Plan.

What is it, I ask you,
that is lacking here?

What is it,
I ask,
that is needed?

Haiku for the American Totality 4/8/24

Eclipse in the sky:
Our worlds align for an hour —
Sun, moon, planet, eye.

Something shared by all,
Coast to coast, straining to see:
Same sliver of sun.

Blazing rim of fire
In each skyward human eye:
Shavings of a star.

Donning dark glasses
We protect our eyes and those
Of people we love.

I wish every child
On this precious earth could look
safely at the sky.

*

Absurdly, today
It felt like the Moon, crossing
The Sun, brought in Spring.

Here in Boston, Mass.
The Eclipse only appeared for
Those who knew to look.

"93 percent" eclipsed,
Without Science to explain:
Just one hazy hour.

If not for the clouds,
What naked eye could sense the
Sun's squinting collapse?

Lifting phone cameras
We capture a miracle:
Moon swallowing Sun.

Millions rush to see
The Sun disappear. (What else
might we help vanish?)

*

A child in Gaza
Looks up from rubble, dead night
Slashed by jet screams.

A child left without
Eyes, or parents, sensing sun
now only by warmth.

Big media lingers
On Big Sky Event, not on
Little bomber planes.

I wish every child
On this precious earth could look
safely at the sky.

Millions celebrate
How a moon can block the sun:
Can our moon block bombs, too?

Bad Insurance Blues

I got to tell somebody
I got the bad insurance blues.
I got to tell somebody
I got the bad insurance blues.
It's got me feeling desperate:
Like I got nothing to lose.

Baby won't stop coughing,
Keeps us up for half the night.
Baby won't stop coughing,
Keeps us up for half the night.
Tried to call the doctor, but
They say our policy ain't right.

I got to tell somebody:
I got the bad insurance blues.
I got to tell somebody:
I got the bad insurance blues.
It's got me feeling desperate:
Like I got nothing to lose.

I called up my provider
When she came down with the flu.
I called up my provider
When she came down with the flu.
By the time they called me back...
She had pneumonia too.

We saw the doctor Sunday
And today I got the bill.
Saw the doc on Sunday
And today I got the bill.
Got me a prescription...
But I can't afford the pills.

I got to tell somebody:
I got the bad insurance blues.
I got to tell somebody:
I got the bad insurance blues.
It's got me feeling desperate:
Like I got nothing to lose.

I heard the news somebody
Went and shot a CEO.
I heard the news somebody
Gone and shot the CEO.
Way I'm feeling lately:
That man got almost what he owed.

Life hits like a crisis,
Comes and knocks off your front door.
Life hits like a crisis,
Comes and knocks off your front door.
Insurance man he walks in
And he pisses on your floor.

I got to tell somebody:
I got the bad insurance blues.
I got to tell somebody:
I got the bad insurance blues.
It's got me feeling desperate:
Like I got nothing to lose.

The house we built, it burned down
Just the other day.
Our only home, it burned down
Just the other day.
Got a note this morning:
Insurance says they will not pay.

Since they wouldn't see me
I went and tracked the head man down.
Boss refused to see me
So I tracked the rich guy down:
The mansion that he lives in
Cost him more than my hometown.

Mama always told me;
Some people take, some people give.
Mama always told me:
People take and people give.
Rich folk, listen up now:
I know just right where you live.

I got to tell somebody:
I got the bad insurance blues.
I got to tell somebody:
I got the bad insurance blues.
It's got me feeling desperate:
Like I got nothing to lose.

This system got me reeling
Like I can't do nothing right
System got me feeling
I just can't to do nothing right.
Sometimes I start to thinking:
All us sick folks must unite.

I got to tell somebody
We got the bad insurance blues.
I'm telling all my people
We got the bad insurance blues.
It's got me feeling sometimes
We got nothing left to lose.

"The Would-be King of Bullshit Springs"

The would-be King of Bullshit Springs—That's him!
His rotten talk could turn a fat cat thin.

The would-be King of Bullshit Springs—Don't fear!
His eye perfume makes real worlds disappear.

That puff of hair, it cast an orange ring.
But spiked into a crown…Might he be king?
He'd won the actual vote, this time around…
Though not quite half the votes, the counters found.
(The largest voting bloc was those who *didn't*—
Many 'cuz their polling place got hidden,
And others more because the opposition
Neglected to present a pot to piss in.)

Yes, "mandate from the people" though he'd call it,
The truth was: people's *silence* let him haul it.
It was, God knows, the path of vote suppression,
That paved the way for Red Don's right succession.

Yet, if you counted only those he LIKED…
His popularity: it *Greatly* spiked!
And so, to shore up his great man condition,
He went to work to silence opposition.

Talk is cheap, they say, and Tweets are cheaper.
Truth was Social: Thus he could defeat Her.
Billionaires pitched in with what they own.
It was their right to rewire all the phones.

The would-be King of Bullshit Springs—That's him!
His rotten talk could turn a fat cat thin.

The would-be King of Bullshit Springs—Don't fear!
His eye perfume makes real worlds disappear.

He somehow sensed the cause of every crash,
Before the ball of fire turned to ash.
His "common sense," it told him what was True
While experts took all night to find a clue.
He Tweeted out the deep dark source of Trouble:
Ignoring any need to sift the rubble.
His wisdom knew no bounds; he just plain *KNEW*
Maybe not the Facts—but what *to Do!*

Such righteous flowing waters he released!
It looked like every wildfire now would cease!
The streaming flood, it glistened in his hand:
Fighting distant fires with unlocked dams!
Never mind the flow he un-impeded
Never reached the place where it was needed.
Or that the waterfalls he made appear
Would guarantee another drought next year.

The would-be King of Bullshit Springs—That's him!
His rotten talk could turn a fat cat thin.

The would-be King of Bullshit Springs—Don't fear!
His eye perfume makes real worlds disappear.

He held the sharpest sharpie in the land.
It turned a wish into a state command.
Who needed Congress passing Legislation
When giant signatures could lead the Nation?
        Or make *some* pesky "nations" *go away,*
Like "Palestine"…Those people would obey,
And drag their bloody tents to Timbuktu
And let their homes be bulldozed like brand new,
and all the flattened schools and mosques of Gaza
be reborn: a seaside tourist plaza--

        OR ELSE, they'd have to face his other palm:
The one he used to bless all Bibi's bombs.

The would-be King of Bullshit Springs—That's him!
His rotten talk could turn a fat cat thin.

The would-be King of Bullshit Springs—Don't fear!
His eye perfume makes real worlds disappear.

If only he could Tweet the people jobs!
Then, surely, they would see his word was God's.
If only words could take the place of work,
Then beaming "aliens," like Captain Kirk,
Back to where they came from, south of here,
Would not make the McMuffins disappear.

If only fruits and veggies picked themselves:
There'd be no images of empty shelves.
If only robot arms could be prepared:
To offer little children daily care,
And change the wise old elders' underwear,
And nail the wood to build the new town square,
And serve up spicy food for friends to share.

The work would still get done: Just ask AI.
The chatbots could send biscuits from the sky.

The would-be King of Bullshit Springs—That's him!
His rotten talk could turn a fat cat thin.

The would-be King of Bullshit Springs—Don't fear!
His eye perfume makes real worlds disappear.

"Flood the zone with shit", he was advised…
And so, a swamp of spectacle devised.

So long as he could keep them on their screens,
He'd be the best-dressed emperor they'd seen.

For now, the key was: keep the people thumbing;
For now, the weather helped, but
Spring was coming...

The would-be King of Bullshit Springs—That's him!
His rotten talk could turn a fat cat thin.

The would-be King of Bullshit Springs—Don't fear!
His eye perfume makes real worlds disappear.

Chants for #TeslaTakedown Protest
Boylston Street, April 2025

Elon Musk! We know you!
Your Grandpa was a Fascist Too!

Hey Elon! We know your name!
Our world is not your video game!

Enough is Enough!
Down with Elon Musk!

Tax the Billionaires!
That Wealth should be Shared!

It's Tax Day! Hurray!
We're Here to Make you Pay!

Put down the chainsaw!
Put down the axes!
We demand you pay your taxes!

Need a Trillion Dollar Cut?
Cut the Pentagon, Not Us!

Hands off!
Medicare!
Hands off!
Medicaid!
Hands off !
Social Security!

Fund What People Need!
Not Corporate Greed!

Ode to DOGE

To end "Waste, Fraud, Abuse,"was what he vowed,
Even if the cuts were not allowed:
Things protected by the Constitution,
Things enshrined in Congress, Institutions.

He'd Fund a gorgeous Tax Cut with the Trillions
Trimmed from sick, poor, loser, fat civilians.
"Waste" was rampant. "Fraud," "Abuse," systemic.
Just count the money spent on the pandemic...
Or count the years the elderly were living--
All those people "taking" and not "giving":
Surely tens of billions could be saved
If retirees could have a few years...shaved.

Trimming Medicare, Social Security
Privatized to restore Market purity,
And gutting Medicaid—this budget third
Would have lifelong effects: they'd thin the herd.

To have so many poor folks live so long:
How did THAT help USA stand strong?
He'd let the winners win—just bet on crypto!—
And let the losers die.
                              But here he'd tiptoe...
For though the truth was he admired the Fuhrer
And how he helped His nation's blood run purer,
He knew This nation wasn't quite yet ready
For open talk of euthanasia. Heady
Stuff this was. Brave heads, cold hearts were
needed; Razor eyes to see the "waste" defeated.

Just cut the programs on which folks depend
And slowly, surely, loser lives would end
Sooner than they would have otherwise—
A year or three or maybe five. There lies

A trillion-dollar savings to be saved
helping greedy grandmas to the grave.
With AI tech his crack team was equipped
To decimate the needy—coupons clipped.

The waste: it wasn't paper. It was people.
Imagine all the savings, once the feeble
Could be purged from all those fraudster programs!
A cleaner way to kill them:
fewer pogroms.

50 million over 65!
Imagine if just ten percent were not alive!
How wise! How cutting edge! to have such guts
To kill poor old folks off to fund tax cuts.
He'd cultivate great fields of golf-course green
In ways America had never seen.
Imagine all the private lawns a'growing
Fertilized, without an old bone showing.

The Would-Be King of Bullshit Springs (2)

The would-be King of Bullshit Springs—That's him!
His rotten talk could turn a fat cat thin.

The would-be King of Bullshit Springs—Don't fear!
His eye perfume makes real worlds disappear.

Vance and Vought, they gave him the Solutions:
And sharpies thicker than ten Constitutions.

Courts would act on what his marker said
Or he would write again—this time in RED.

No court appeals, no idle legal threats:
He longed to write his name with bayonets.

So if the federal workers wouldn't listen,
He'd show them how an iron man's will could glisten.

And if they told him *Stop* and came to get him;
Hegseth's Army troopers wouldn't let them.

And if ol' wild man Pete can't find his phone,
He'd shoot the bums himself —
Defend the Throne.

And if a Judge sent agents to his door?
That was what Pam Bondi's goons were for.

And if mass protests grew so vast and wide
That White House walls were swamped from
every side,

And Mar-a-Lago's gates clogged up with losers:
Lazy, poorslobs, wokesters, dregs and boozers-

And all the roads were blocked by those who'd
boo him,
He bought a special Tesla to drive *through* them.

And if the whole damn Country fell to Hell
They still would never lock him in that cell.

He'd ride a rocket ship to meet on Mars
And plot with Elon—Colonize the stars!

And if denounced by, say, the Pope in Rome,
He'd buy a church, or two…or build his own!

The would-be King of Bullshit Springs—That's him!
His rotten talk could turn a fat cat thin.

The would-be King of Bullshit Springs—Don't fear!
His eye perfume makes real worlds disappear.

To be God's voice on Earth: it was his goal.
And those who didn't like it? Heads would roll.

His orders could—like that!—remake The World!
Just see the brand-new maps that he unfurled!

No more, our Gulf be soiled with "Mexico":
AMERICA: as pure as Texaco.

Greenland would be next. Its name—obscene!
Melt off all that ice—He'd show them *green*!

No more! those rainbow flags the commies flew;
He liked things black and white:red white & blue.

No more! this gender fluid youth revolt;
He'd shock them back to true Sex with one jolt.

No more! these students publishing their thoughts!
They'd bow their heads and *listen* while they're taught.

No more! these dirty tents, this campus riot.
He knew what schooling meant. It meant:
Be Quiet.

(Not that he'd been one to sit and study.
Who needs books when all the world is putty?)

(The World, it could be shaped
by His two hands.
He'd mold the people's lives,
like beach-bought sand….)

The would-be King of Bullshit Springs—That's him!
His rotten talk could turn a fat cat thin.

The would-be King of Bullshit Springs—Don't fear!
His eye perfume makes real worlds disappear.

The Would-Be King of Bullshit Springs (3)

But here's the thing with sand:
some grains get through.

And here and there
some stuck inside his shoe,
Or somehow got inside his socks,
and itched
Enough to make him stomp—
Sonofabitch!

He hated how they stuck between his toes--
Made him want to thrash at all his foes.
And if sand grains kept gathering down there,
He couldn't sit; they'd breach his underwear.
And if the sand piled up, like falling snow,
Each floating flake stuck to the one below,
Before long he'd be covered to the ass,
A frozen statue in an hourglass,
Choking, coughing, overcome by sand
A victim in his own quick-conquered land.

[*Stocks were falling and the people rising*
It wasn't any time to start revising.
His motto was: Why buy when you can steal?
And always tilt the table when you deal.]

His Tariff Package would bring Liberation
Starting with one long standing ovation…
At least from those invited to attend
and vetted to make sure their knees can't bend
Except of course when told to. That's the thing:
You need them to stand strong,
Yet kiss the ring.

The would-be King of Bullshit Springs—That's him!
His rotten talk could turn a fat cat thin.

The would-be King of Bullshit Springs—Don't fear!
His eye perfume makes real worlds disappear.

And then while sifting sand he felt
a *bite*...
And then another.
Couldn't see them:
Mites?
And then across his arm he felt some *bumps*...

At first, he thought the redness might be mea-
sles? Maybe *mumps?*
But these were very different kinds of *lumps*:
Pointy balls that bulged and grew to *stumps*
And then, these swelling *pods*, their hearts did
THUMP—-
And from them *popped*
a hundred little *Trumps!*

Puff-haired, spray-tanned, mean-mouthed
beach-side minions
(Kind of like that classic scene from *Gremlins*
Except these popping fur balls weren't so cute
And had but one foul purpose: *grab the loot.*)

Each tyrant spud stretched wide to claim Dominion,
Declaring as The Law his own Opinion.

And suddenly, beach-trolls were everywhere:
Lifeguard-like, except without the stare:
Looking not to ocean waves for strife
Or to bring back a struggling swimmer's life.
Instead, they sought to stare just where they stood,
And hold the pose just like a Master would.

Binoculars are what a lifeguard wears
To see not just what's *here* but what is *there*.
And microscopes are what the scientists use
To figure out the *specks* within the *ooze*.

But these foul gremlins sprouted other tools:
A kind of squinting glass that's made for fools,
A fractured prism crystal that, looked through,
Melts all human flesh to glop and goo.
And if it caught the blazing sun, just so,
Could forge a laser beam to blind a foe,
Or start a blaze, just like the headman ordered:
Have all pesky insects drawn and quartered.

All the rising sand, the swirling gnats
--All the world a beach, the beach a vat--
The beach-born bastards took to melting down
The world of sand: to fashion glass from ground.

And once 1000 Trumplings lined the beach
Victory would be so trumpily in reach.
For once the land was flattened
Like a slum block in Manhattan:
Melted down, the sand grew clearer,
And when done,
he'd have a *Mirror*:
One smooth surface, one Reflection:
And one Face:
Now THAT's perfection.

(Yes, whether it was Gaza
or t'was Greenland…
The truth was what he longed for
was *More-Me-Land*.)

The would-be King of Bullshit Springs—That's him!
His rotten talk could turn a fat cat thin.

53

The would-be King of Bullshit Springs—Don't fear!
His eye perfume makes real worlds disappear.

But the water: it got hotter
Steaming by the sizzling sand.
Mother Nature, though he'd fought her
Yet her throat slipped from his hands.
Ink black contracts said he'd bought her
But those depths had other plans …

CHANT SHEET for "Kill the Cuts!" Rally
April 8, 2025

Down with Tyranny!
Up with **Knowledge**!
Don't Let Trump
Destroy your **College**!

Hands off **Students**!
Hands off **Science**!
We Say **No**! to
Trump Compliance!

Free Rumeysa Now!
Free Mahmoud Now!

When I say "Free Them" you say: "Now!"
Free them!   Now!
Free them!   Now!

Fight for Freedom!
Now's the Time!
Speaking Up
Is not a crime!

Faculty, Grads, Workers, **Unite**!
They say CUT BACKS
We say: **Fight**!

Staff, Students, Teachers, **Unite**!
They say : CUT BACKS
We say: **FIGHT**!

On Frost and Fire

Some say we'll change the world with love,
Some say with hate.
To make real what we're dreaming of
I hold with those who lead with love.

But if to smash the current state
Is all that we have left in mind,
I do not doubt the force of hate
though often blind
is also great.

(with apologies to R.F.)

So Haitians are eating American pets?*

Do they lure Fluffy
Into the alleyway
Behind the public park
(Where you meet your hired sweetheart
after dark)
And tear out her fleecy white belly
With a sugary machete smuggled in
Without a proper permit?

I hear that Haitian migrants are eating your pets.

Do they pounce from behind
Trimmed suburban hedges,
Tossing manicured poodles by the tail
into airtight sacks
gasping for air
to be rendered Meat
for Monsters to eat
in some Satanic basement?

Well,
I've asked around for these secret raiders
Hoping that maybe snatching
yipping designer dogs
And clobbering slobber hounds
behind the ears
when they least expect it
Might be some kind of training run--
          Midnight practice
for taking down more worthy predators:
Two-legged, wide-striding American beasts;
Gold-necked crypto-crank tech bros,
Neo-feudal overseers
filling galactic gas tanks

with hot air
sucked from the breeching lips
of billions below them:
a vast human ocean
treading water
to survive just another day
until tomorrow.

Yes, I've looked around for these rebels.
But no such *Cacos* have I yet found:
No *Boukman.*
No *Mackandal.*
No *Charlemagne Peralte.*
Marble memories of *Toussaint*, maybe.
But hardly a whisper of his brother *Moise*
      (Who called for the land
        to belong to the tiller).

All the Haitians in America I know
Are too busy working their asses off
To plot insurrection:
Holding down multiple jobs
Taking night classes to improve their English
and earn their degrees
      And maybe record that album.
Too busy singing in church on Sunday
Too busy taking care of people
To plan a proper Big Dog-snatching.

The Haitians I know barely have time to sleep,
Half-zombified by an American Dream
Their phone alarms yank them back
from grasping even with dream-hands,
stiff collared into uniforms
subway cars and traffic jams:
Never to be late
to serve the Dunkins America runs on,

to change sick abandoned grandmother bedpans
to make sure forgetful old men take their pills
to mind children when their parents go away
to drive people to work when they're running late
to bag groceries for harried shoppers
(and at the same time ever on their phones
checking on the folks back home
sending a slice of each paycheck back to those
who cannot leave the island, who need help,
loved ones whose wretched condition
on that once-succulent colony pumped dry
for foreign profit
is both the ultimate indictment of this system
and yet also makes
60 hours of wage labor a week in the USA
look like luck).

The Haitians I know cradle
newborn babies with love,
Offer gems of human wisdom
      Woch nan dlo pa konnen mizè wóch nan
      soléy. Tout moun se moun.

And take care of cats and dogs
like anyone else would:
clicking tongues
      beckoning black white
           spotted pets across the room
                 to get
                 their necks
          scratched.

And so when ICE thugs raid the homes
of these Haitian neighbors,
separating mothers from children,
throwing handcuffs on the wrists of healers,
And knees into the necks of deacons,

Do they make sure to find a good home
for each dog and cat
They leave behind without a loyal, loving owner
now shoved into an unmarked van?

Yes, after they've kicked down
the alien door
and reclaimed for America
some rented floor
of an apartment owned by an absent landlord,
After ignoring the screams of the frightened
pets howling to keep them out,
Do the agents then take off their masks
and pull out a pad of paper and pencil
to carefully consult
the list of dog- and cat-lovers of America,
making sure each traumatized orphaned animal
finds the loving American home it deserves,
Where it will receive the nourishing food
clean water
and safe haven
that all god's creatures require?

Or,
do they just kick the pets aside,

Or shoot them dead,
for instance,
        if the dogs look like they might
have it in them
to bite

or just for fun

because they can

                and who will stop them?

*Offered with a hat-tip to Jimmy Santiago Baca https://apoemaday.tumblr.com/post/720307156334854144/so-mexicans-are-taking-jobs-from-americans and a middle finger to James David Vance: https://www.npr.org/2024/09/10/nx-s1-5107320/jd-vance-springfield-ohio-haitians-pets

P.S. Re: Those Lost Pets

Could it have been that the toxic maw
Of the shuttered factory
Gone south
Swallowed them?

"Rib Cages at Twilight"

I hold my toddler tight
In the evening before we start
her bed-time routine:
My only daughter,
Sweet Lila Joy,
not quite 3 years old.

I hold her in my lap on the rocking chair
as she eats cornbread with both hands
and curls her feet
and watches a Disney cartoon musical
we've seen a dozen times at least,
while through an Apple airbud
I listen with one ear
To the latest news
Via *Democracy Now!*:
The latest news
from Gaza:
66000 children facing severe malnutrition
Hundreds already on the verge of starvation
Record numbers of child amputees
undergoing surgeries
without anesthesia
Dozens of people killed before dawn just today
Many of them
As every day now: Children
Lying asleep in their makeshift beds
or sitting on their parents' laps
or standing in line for food
or lying in the hospital for treatment
when US-Israeli bombs blasted their lives
incinerated their entire families
sheared off their limbs.

My arms around Lila,
I feel her rib cage with my fingers:
That ripple accordion of life
Up and down her side.
Her ribs, padded and buffered
as they should be,
a healthy layer of baby fat
and soft skin
beneath cozy pajama flannel.

Lila starts a big yawn,
tiny hands balling into fists,
and I feel her rib cage expand
massively against my cupped hand
Arching and stretching to take in as much
Of this world's air as she possibly can
before expelling the breath
With the sweetest sigh I know.

Yes, it's time to stop the movie for tonight.
Lila may complain a bit.
But we both know we can finish it tomorrow.

About the Author:

Joseph G. Ramsey, Ph.D. is an educator, scholar, critic, organizer, activist, and parent, residing in Boston, MA. A rank-in-file activist in the Faculty Staff Union (FSU/MTA) at UMass Boston, Joe also works with the nationwide coalition Higher Ed Labor United (HELU) where he chairs the Contingency Task Force. Editor of four book-length anthologies including *Scholactivism: Reflections on Transforming Praxis*, Joe's scholarly research focuses on U.S. and African American literary radicalisms. A longstanding member of the Marxist Literary Group, Joe also helps organize the Richard Wright Society, and is nearing completion of a book about Wright's critical communism, and another on Wright's haiku. His essays and articles have appeared in numerous places, including: *The Nation, Counterpunch, Jacobin, The Chronicle of Higher Education, Inside Higher Ed, Dispatches from the Poetry Wars, Monthly Review, Cultural Logic, Mediations, Salon, Socialism & Democracy*, and *Science & Society* (forthcoming), as well as several edited book volumes. You can reach him at jgramsey AT gmail.com.

www.ingramcontent.com/pod-product-compliance
Lightning Source LLC
Chambersburg PA
CBHW031235120626
46545CB00003B/1130